C000246607

TITANIA'S WISHING SPELLS

HARMONY

TITANIA HARDIE

QUADRILLE

What is harmony and what does it mean to us?
A life, or a moment, or a day spent without discord?
A balance of individual energies that together make
up a beautifully chimed wholeness? Perhaps paying
attention to avoiding bitter or strident notes coming
between ourselves and our lovers, families and
work associates. Even an invitation to look at the
world through someone else's eyes, and then strive
for a balance, a blending of colours that makes a
sympathetic palette.

The best perfumes are blended by achieving a perfect balance
of scented 'notes' – usually a high, a middle and a low note.
Sometimes one will be a keynote and dominate, but the others
will surround it in perfect olfactory harmony, often so that we
don't even realise the other notes are there.

These little wishing spells are dedicated to creating a rainbow
of feelings and thoughts that blend in with others; we concentrate
on our power to create a harmonious home or work life. On a
grander scale, we see how we can make a rainbow of different
coloured thoughts and ideas, different belief systems, or reactions
to things, chime better with our own. It begins as we emanate

harmony from within ourselves. Define harmony for yourself as you will, without losing sight of the concept of well-tuned voices without discord.

If we wish really hard for something we can make it ours. My grandmother cautioned me from childhood to select my wishes carefully, for they would come true. These wishing rituals are remnants of very old customs and with a child-like heart and enthusiasm you can make them work wonders.

Wish well and wisely.

Titania Hardie

AMBER

Pretty amber beads have been accorded many
powers, including the ability to ward off colds and
respiratory complaints. They are also known for the
power to heal rifts and attract powerful positivity.

When you see a particularly clear full moon on a very bright,
starlit night, take a piece of amber and rub it on what are known
as the 'planetary pulses' – the temples, the throat, the wrists, the
insteps and the throne of the heart (between the breast bones).
As you do so, close your eyes and wish for a perfect balance of
energies in those departments of your life – your mind, your
words to others, your ability to work and earn, your physical
and sexual energy and your capacity for love.

Keep the amber as an amulet and hang it around your neck if
you like. It attracts a long period of harmonious relationships
and can be renewed at the next bright moon.

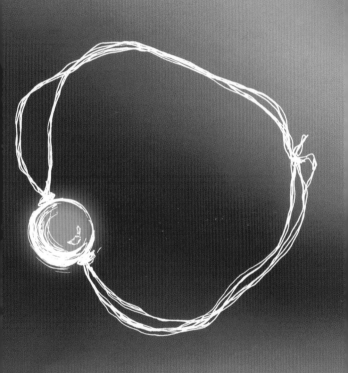

Champagne cork

This ritual is quite recent in the canon of magical practices. For a long time cork was held to be very lucky because it floats, but the association with champagne is undoubtedly connected with its inherent properties of luxury and sparkle.

When a bottle of champagne is given to you, open the bottle and ask everyone in the room to wish for prosperity and a harmonious life ahead. Ask everyone to kiss the cork, then slice it open at the small end. Place a coin inside the split, forcing it down well. It is now important to keep this cork until you receive the next bottle of champagne. It is also lucky to inscribe the date on each cork and keep them. The cork itself becomes a talisman of harmony and good spirits.

FIRST FOOT

This old tradition, which stretches at least as far
back as the Romans, states that you must take your
best foot forward into a house or a new venture.
The 'first foot' chosen was always that of a man,
but nowadays equality would allow a woman the
role too, I think!

On New Year's Eve this custom is still observed in Scotland
to welcome in the new year and bring prosperity and harmony
to the gathered friends and family. Traditionally, at the last
hour of the evening, between 11 p.m. and midnight, someone
nominated as the 'first foot' must bring into the house a piece
of coal and a bough of an evergreen plant (but never a piece of
yew). These tokens usher in the powers of nature, symbolising
warmth and plenty, with the evergreen bestowing harmony
between the inmates of the house. Once these are in place –
usually beside a hearth – everyone must make a wish for
prosperity, and the coming year should be joyful and serene.

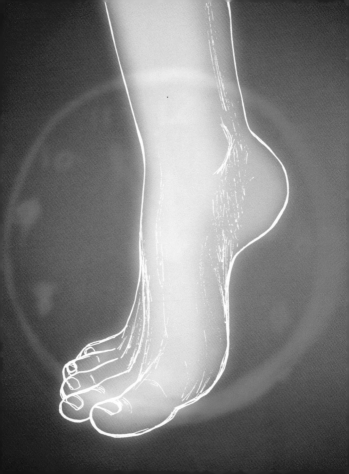

GARLIC

This is especially lucky if you see a green sprouting knuckle of garlic. Long held as the most efficacious and potent protector of all (an idea Bram Stoker seized on to great effect), garlic will not only keep away vampires and witches, but more importantly, will ensure that all negativity and ill luck is held at arm's length.

When you have just moved into a new home, or otherwise on All Hallow's Eve or May Eve, take a bulb of garlic with any hint of green on it, wrap it in a silken square (such as a handkerchief) and place it in the thatch (if you're lucky enough to have a thatched roof), or in the rafters, or upon the roof near the chimney. Imagine a rainbow of harmonious, blended light encircling your home, and wish hard for harmony and happiness under its roof. The garlic will keep the goblins away!

STOCKING

This is an old favourite. In a world before tights, stockings were a wonderful omen of love and luck, of prosperity and happiness. This will work best with a hold-up thigh-high stocking, when you wear it on a special occasion.

If your stocking wrinkles and refuses to stay pulled up no matter what you do to it, your loved one is thinking of you. Touching the wrinkle, make a huge wish for harmony and joy between you and the one you love. See happiness and perfect amity reigning in your house for years to come. When you take the stocking off, tie it in a simple knot and wish again. Joy and harmony are yours for the asking.

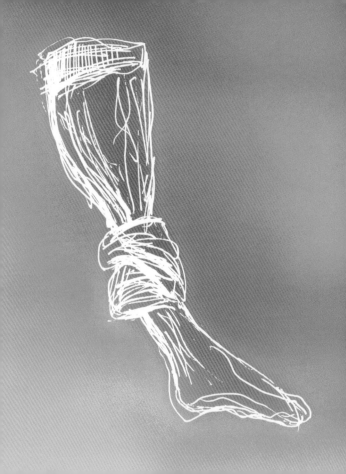

Apron

You may have heard the old saying that if your apron strings become untied, someone is thinking lovingly of you. This may happen when you have had a rift with someone dear to you and they wish to make it up. There is a short wish ritual that you can perform if this happens.

If your apron strings become undone of their own accord, immediately turn around once and make a wish to put things back together on a more harmonious footing with someone who has been at odds with you. Silently mouth your wish to make this quarrel up, then quickly and gently tap a glass to make a short ringing sound. Within the week, your friend or loved one will meet you halfway towards renewed concord.

MINCE PIE 2

There are many stories of luck and prosperity attending breads, buns, pies and puddings. Mince pies are among the easiest to deal with.

Throughout the season of Yuletide, whenever you are visiting a friend, bear these thoughts in mind. Every time you are served a mince pie in a different house (or restaurant), make a wish as you bite into it. Make a generous wish for health and happiness, but above all for harmony among your friends, loves and family. You will have a month of bliss for each mince pie that you eat in a different place. Try to work up an appetite!

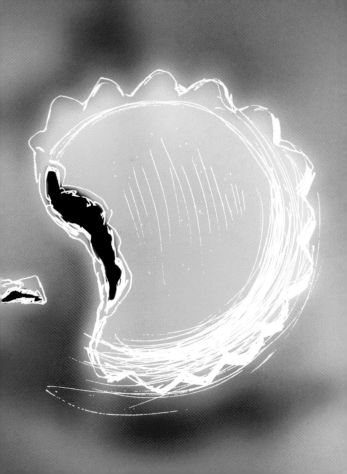

OATMEAL

This is an old custom that my grandmother set great store by.

When you move into a new house, or visit someone in a newish home, take with you three things: some oatmeal, some salt and an iron key. These should be kept somewhere they won't be much disturbed, and wished on just once for the following: Enough to eat, Emotion enough to cry tears of happiness and Endurance enough to survive all tests. Together, these three Es will bring harmony to your life.

My grandmother felt that salt was the most important gift and would give some away to those who left the house, to ensure that they took no luck away and to perpetuate good feeling and fortune. So always keep plenty of salt in the house – even if you never plan to use it.

PEACOCK FEATHER

My grandmother worried about peacock feathers
as they were once thought to have the evil eye.
However, peacocks themselves are the birds of Juno,
most powerful goddess, so if a girl is given or finds
a peacock feather, here is what she should do.

Take the plume and place it near an instrument for making
music: a piano or violin is usual (but a CD player would do).
As you do so, say: "Dream and vivacity lives in your colour,
bring me harmonious love from another." A love of true
harmony and peace will envelop you, and this may last as
long as you have the feather.

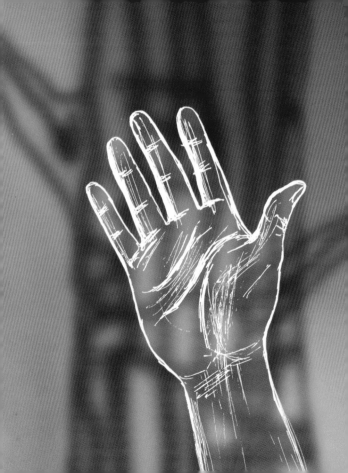

ITCHY PALM

Everyone knows, of course, that an itchy right palm presages luck with money. Did you also know you could do a short ritual with an itchy palm?

When your right palm itches, it is sure to mean luck. To make sure it works properly, and brings luck in business and plenty of work to do, you should rub your hand on a tree. As you're doing so, say "Rub my hand against wood, 'Tis sure to come good." Cover the right hand with the left, still against the wood, to ensure that you have harmonious relations with all those with whom you work.

SALT 2

If you've been having a run of problems and a series of arguments with your beloved, try this.

Put a handful of salt into a silver-coloured bucket and place it inside the front door. When you are together, take a pinch of the salt from the bucket and toss it over your loved one's shoulder, saying: "No more salt and tears spilled." Ask your love to do the same. Then take a pinch each and toss it out of the front door. Keep the salt in the bucket for a week, and all should be harmonious and loving for a month at least.

Midsummer

On Midsummer Day, magic is afoot everywhere. This ritual involves a piece of coal or charcoal, taken carefully from a barbecue.

Take long-handled tongs and grasp a piece of smouldering coal. Ask the live coal to bring you plenty of blessings, then bury it safely in the ground, covering it over well with the earth. (If you live in a hot climate, make sure you bury the coal with enough earth, in a cool damp place, not to present any fire hazards.) As you bury the coal or charcoal, imagine a spark of warmth from the earth, and wish for amity and accord everywhere around you.

Mark the place where you buried the coal, and within a month, plant some flowers there. When they bloom pick one regularly to ensure blessings and harmony throughout the summer and autumn.

CRICKET

If a long-legged fellow hops into your home, look
what he brings.

When you discover a cricket in your house, ask Mr Cricket to
chirp out a song of harmony, peace and plenty. Be hospitable,
and do not goad him to leave. If he sings in your home, he will
bring lots of luck and good feeling between the people who live
there. He should leave only when he himself is ready – through
an open window or door. Always be especially kind to visitors
such as bees, crickets, beetles or ladybirds – they bring luck and
happiness to your home.

HARES AND RABBITS

My mother never let a month go by without doing this one. If she ever forgot, she would worry about troubles in the month ahead.

In the last hour of the last day of the month, say softly before going to bed: "Hares, hares, hares." Make a quiet wish for harmony on all fronts: in your home, your job, with your family, your lover and in your daily tasks.

In the morning, on the first day of the new month, before you say anything to anyone at all, you must say: "Rabbits, rabbits, rabbits." Now wish quickly again for a harmonious month ahead. Your month should be quite lucky and free from doubts.

BABY'S HANDS

This may not happen very often, but if a baby is born with its hands open, it is said that it will have a life of plenty. This little ritual is rather sweet to do, if a baby is born into your house or family, or that of a friend, with open hands.

Rub your finger over the baby's palms (they will close over your finger), and make a wish for prosperity and health to the child, and harmony and peace to the family. The baby born with open hands gives generously to its family, and presages good spirit and cheer within the household.

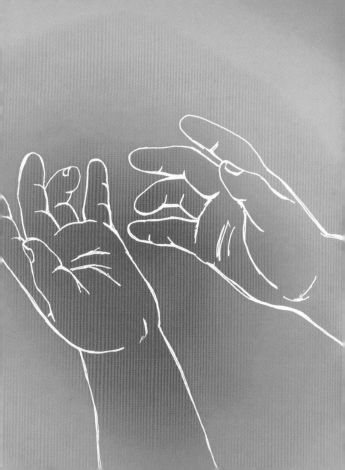

Door

This is a ritual you should observe if you want to
guarantee harmony in a new marriage.

When leaving for her wedding, the bride must contrive
somehow to leave her door open. For security, it might be best
to have someone stay in the house during this time, but for the
peace and blessings of the nuptials to enter the life of the bride,
her door should, at least, be left unlocked. To ensure that the
day itself is harmonious the bride must not look back once she
has left the house, but should quickly close her eyes and wish
strongly for a lifetime of good fortune and marital felicity.

DONKEY

This may seem a strange choice, but donkeys have long been considered to be lucky and mystical little beings. A pet donkey is often kept on a farm just for the peace and accord it brings. To re-establish harmony among warring factions within the household or workplace, try this.

Buy a toy donkey and wrap it in rose-coloured cloth. On the night of a bright new moon, take the donkey out of the cloth, and present it to the moon, asking for her silvery beams to bless the world around you.

Take the toy donkey and put it somewhere unusual in the home. Place a rose-coloured flower next to it, and wish for harmony among your friends and family, and protection for your home. Keep your donkey safe, and adorn it with a fresh flower whenever you feel the need to allay feelings of anxiety between people in your home.

FERN

Here's a way to find out whether the year ahead will be prosperous and full of harmony in your love life.

At midsummer, or on St Swithin's Day (July 14), take a nice fat fern stalk and cut through it, slantwise, near to the root. Close your eyes and wish for luck and domestic happiness in the year ahead, and as you turn the stalk upward to inspect it, see what shape is inside the stalk. You are especially blessed and will have luck and harmony for a twelvemonth if the shape made by the veins clearly resembles an oak tree, which is a strong possibility. Sometimes the veins will make a letter, and you should observe this as an omen and a direction to watch for as a lucky portent for the future.

IRON POKER

This ritual works from the idea that iron is strong, reliable and lucky.

Whenever there has been any disturbance in the home or the family, an iron poker must be placed in the corner of an outside-facing wall, to 'shore up our strength and restore harmony'. Touching the iron for luck, at any time, would be sure to safeguard an important meeting or appointment, and make certain it went ahead with amity and good feeling. This could be immensely important before a first date.

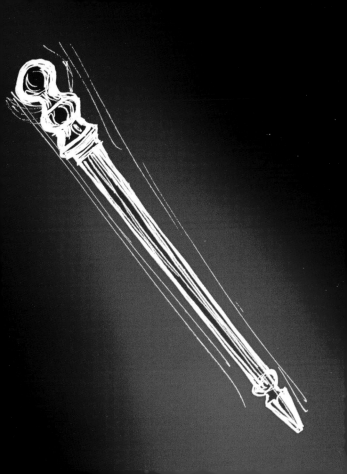

Silver sixpence

Never mind the onset of all European currency being replaced by the euro, finding an old sixpence or silver coin is becoming a near impossibility. Here's what to do if one turns up unexpectedly in an old drawer or cupboard.

A silver sixpence is very lucky. If you come across one, or come to that any silver coin, place it first on your nose, then on your forehead, then lastly, toss it over your left shoulder, disregarding where it may land. As you throw it, wish heartily for complete felicity and harmony in your life, and especially with one special person you have in mind. The finding of the silver coin already presages great luck for a twelvemonth.

Rainbow

When you see a rainbow stretching over your house, or in the road before you, perform this little ritual.

Stop and blow the rainbow a kiss, and thank Juno and her peacocks. Now you must quickly make the first unselfish wish you can think of. Then immediately look around you for any little coloured objects that will make up the colours of the rainbow: look for flowers, leaves, little coloured stones or string, anything at all. As soon as you can, put the objects into an envelope, seal it with a kiss, and wish again.

You should have thirty peaceful days and loving nights, as a result of your unselfish thoughts.

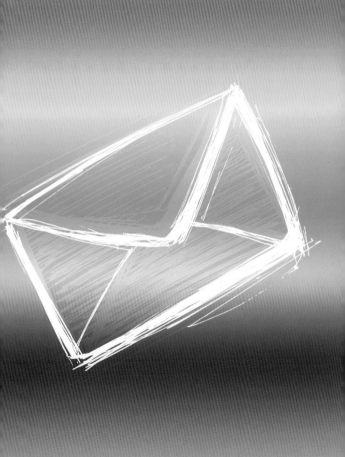

ELEPHANTS

These are regarded as among the very luckiest of
animals. An elephant charm is second to none as a
lucky token. My mother always added the tip that
the elephant's trunk should be pointing upwards
(like a horseshoe) so that the luck stays with you.

To ensure harmonious feelings among those with whom you
work, and especially to ensure that the business itself flourishes,
find an elephant charm (a small silver charm, as for a bracelet,
would be ideal) and sew it into the hem of a curtain or blind
near where you sit at work. Of course, you could also do this at
home. Position the elephant within the hem so that it is facing
the nearest door. In this way the elephant will know what is
going on, monitor all visitors and encourage only the best things
to come through that door. For an important meeting or date,
rub the elephant within the fabric and wish for success.

RHYME

Rhymes are a sure sign of making magic that will work: the words themselves will do the enchanting, literally. Here's what to do if you suddenly make a rhyme with someone else, without having intended to do so.

When your last sentence rhymes with the first sentence someone else utters, or vice versa, touch hands, palm to palm, and say: "That's harmony, for thee and me." Write the rhyming words themselves in your diary for the day, or on a calendar page, and wish for peace in the world.

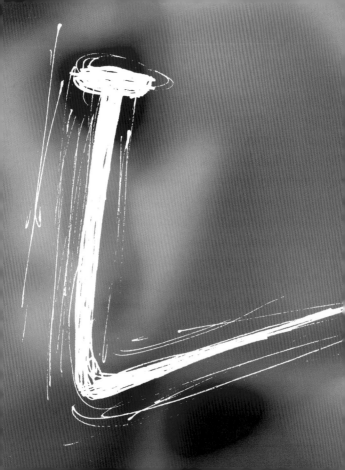

CROOKED PIN

Perhaps because nothing is perfect except divinity, anything crooked (that would usually be straight) is considered lucky. This belief is usually applied to a pin, but a nail or a horseshoe or even a crooked stick would be appropriate.

If you come across something in the street, which would normally be straight, but is crooked, make a wish for a lover or friend who has strayed from you to be reunited in good feeling with you again: "My line with you has gone askew, now end the feud and make us new." Put the pin in your lapel, and expect harmonious relations to be restored soon.

TWELFTH NIGHT

This is an important wish ritual to observe for a year of good fortune and peacefulness.

On the eve of Twelfth Night (January 5), in company with friends, take the wassail bowl out to twelve trees or bushes in the garden, or to a neighbouring orchard. The wassail bowl (any large bowl will do) should contain some cider and some small pieces of toasted bread, as well as a few wintry flowers and spices (cinnamon is especially lucky).

Sprinkle some of the wassail on twelve trees, trying to find at least one fruit tree, and say: "Here's to thee, old fruit tree, and when thou mayst blossom and blow; Hat's full, and cap's full, and my own pockets too. Peace and good will be among you."

This ensures a certain peace among the revellers until next Twelfth Night, and peace, besides, because there is enough on the table to provide for their needs.

COMFREY

When you have lost your feelings of spark and harmony with the world around you, try this.

Bind two comfrey leaves gently together with a pink ribbon and place under your pillow. If you are at odds with someone in particular, write their name between the leaves on a slip of paper. Wish hard for a return of good will and harmony.

Morning will bring you a new optimism, and probably also, a message of accord.

SUNWISE

Sunwise means 'clockwise', the direction of the sun, from east to west is best. This little performance will bring a harmony of pleasures to any new beginning – a voyage, business, house or love affair.

On the morning you are to begin something new, walk three times around in a circle 'sunwise' at your own door, and then three times around in a circle similarly at the door of the blossoming situation. Wish for a rainbow of promise, and imagine one stretching over your head. Now enter the office or the home, or embark on the trip or the love affair. You will have harmonious protection from the divine.

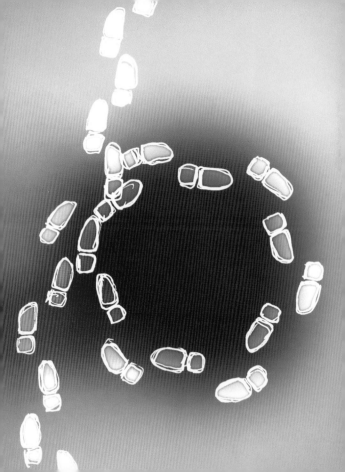

WHITE HORSE

After you have suffered an illness or a period of
depression, the luckiest omen you can see is a white
horse running free.

If you spot one running in a field or paddock, immediately place
all the fingertips of one hand against the fingertips of the other.
Press them against each other, and say: "My strength has been
tested, my fortitude also. The white horse running free sets my
spirits free besides. My inner harmony will be restored. Blessed
be." Blow a kiss to the horse, and wish for a real return of your
feelings of personal strength and control.

Heather

This is usually regarded as a very unlucky plant to
bring into the house, but white heather is different.

If you are given a piece of white heather, take it to a darkish
corner in your home. Light a small white candle beside it,
then wish for luck in your dealings and harmony in all your
relationships. Allow the heather to dry completely, then keep
a sprig to brighten the darkest corner.

If you are thinking of planting a heather plant near your front
door or path, make sure it is white.

Purse

Best for last: I've kept this lovely little ritual for the end. It is one I always try to do.

Whenever you are setting forth on any kind of new adventure – a new place to live, or to work, or to study, or to stay, or to be with new people, or friends, or a new lover – make sure you take a little purse and a piece of string, and a wish that you speak into the inside of the purse. If you do, you will never be without the money you truly need, friends enough for pleasure and strength, and a harmonious life wherever you are heading.

This makes a good gift for someone going away; the string can be tied into a circle and placed inside the purse.

First published in 2002 by
Quadrille Publishing Limited
Alhambra House
27-31 Charing Cross Road
London WC2H 0LS

Reprinted in 2002

EDITOR Anne Furniss
DESIGN Jim Smith
PRODUCTION Tracy Hart, Vincent Smith

British Library Cataloguing in Publication Data
A catalogue record for this book is available
from the British Library

ISBN 1 903845 89 0

Printed in Hong Kong

10 9 8 7 6 5 4 3 2